Catalogue and e-commerce
Our catalogue of books and other products can be consulted on:
http://www.msm-editions.fr
http://www.msm-publishers.com
These are business sites with secure on-line payment.

© **MSM** , 1991, 2005.

65500 Vic-en-Bigorre – France
Tel.: (33) 05 62 31 68 01, Fax.: (33) 05 62 31 68 08
e-mail : contact@msm-editions.fr

Dépôt légal: June 2006
ISBN 978-2-3508-0009-7

Printed by Llob 3, Barberà del Vallès – Spain (february 2013)

Bernadette

The child who saw

Drawings: Gemma Sales
Text: Michel Vaidis

Historical and Religious Advisor: Father Joseph Bordes
English Translation Superior: Father John Lochran

MSM

At the time when Lourdes was just a village nestling at the foot of the Pyrenees...

A miller, François Soubirous, his wife, Louise and their three children, Bernadette, Toinette and Jean Marie lived in a pretty mill by a stream which ran at the foot of the castle of Lourdes.

They were happy and loved each other dearly. They were kind-hearted and helped the poor. The miller provided flour even to customers who could not pay for it.

"You can pay me when you can..."

One year there was a drought and the harvest of corn was very bad. The miller produced less flour and could not pay the rent for the mill.

"I'll settle up with you later..." he promised the land-lord.

"No! Either you pay or you go!", the latter replied without pity.

So, sick at heart, François and his family had to leave the mill of happiness.

François and his family found shelter in a small, dark and cold room which had once been a prison and which was known as the "cachot" (meaning "dungeon").

François hired himself out as a labourer but his wage was not enough to feed the whole family. So Louise and even Bernadette had to work.
Despite their extreme poverty, they remained hopeful and prayed...
But one morning a new misfortune fell upon them.
Two policemen knocked at the door.
"François! The baker says you have stolen a sack of flour! Follow us!"
François was led to prison. But as he was not the culprit he was freed eight days later.

In order to have one less mouth to feed, Bernadette was sent to a farm in the village of Bartrès. There she looked after the sheep with the help of her little dog Pigou. Separated from her sister and her brother, she became bored and wanted to go home. Her father, who often came to see her, advised her to stay,
"Here you eat well, you are better off here than at the cachot... "
But Bernadette, who was now fourteen years old, wanted to go to school and learn the catechism. In order to rejoin her family, she found a good excuse,
"The parish priest of Lourdes wants me to make my first communion!"

On this Thursday 11th February 1858, it was very cold... In the cachot the fire had gone out in the fireplace. Bernadette, Toinette and their friend, Baloume went out to collect some dead wood in a grotto which was used as a pig-pen. This place was called Massabielle and in order to get there they had to cross a small stream bare-footed. The water was icy cold. Bernadette hesitated.

As she started to take off her socks and shoes a small breeze made her raise her head towards the grotto. She saw a young lady appear in a faint light who was dressed all in white. She was very frightened and clutched her rosary. As the Apparition smiled at her, making the sign of the Cross, Bernadette was no longer afraid and started to pray with her. On seeing her kneeling down, Toinette made fun of her.

On the way home, Bernadette was very surprised when her sister and Baloume told her they had not seen anything. Toinette was curious and begged her sister,

"Tell me what you saw! I won't repeat it to anyone."

Once back at the cachot, Toinette could not keep her tongue from wagging.
"Bernadette says she saw a 'White Lady'".

On hearing this, Mama Louise was afraid that another misfortune would strike the family. She became angry and scolded Bernadette, "You saw nothing. You saw a white rock. I forbid you to return there!" However, the following Sunday after mass, Bernadette returned to the grotto with her father's permission. The young lady appeared to her for the second time.

For the third Apparition a lady, wanting to solve this mystery, accompanied Bernadette. Following her advice Bernadette asked the young lady to write her name. The Apparition smiled and replied,

"That is not necessary... but would you be so kind as to come here for fifteen days... I do not promise happiness in this world but in the other..."

Bernadette promised.

The whole town was talking about Bernadette. Some people said it was the Blessed Virgin who appeared to her. People, now curious, came to see what was happening. Every day there were more and more people at the grotto. The police superintendent became worried and had Bernadette brought to his office to question her severely,

"So you see the Blessed Virgin, do you?"

"I didn't say that I had seen the Blessed Virgin. I saw a small young lady, she has a white dress tied with a blue belt, a white veil on her head and a yellow rose on each foot. She holds a rosary in her hands."

The superintendent did not believe Bernadette, he became angry and wanted to make her admit that she had made all of this story up. But Bernadette stood up to him.

Despite the police superintendent, who had asked her father to forbid her to go to the grotto, Bernadette returned there every morning.

At the eighth Apparition, Bernadette's eyes filled with tears. She was asked why she was crying.

"The young lady was unhappy. She told me to pray for sinners..." she replied.

The next day, for the ninth Apparition, a crowd of curious people were watching Bernadette when, suddenly, she began to walk on all fours. Going to the back of the grotto, she kissed the ground. There she dug a hole at the bottom of which she found water. She took some in her cupped hands but it was so dirty that she threw it away. At the fourth attempt she drank a mouthful with distaste and then she washed her face with it. Then, with her cheeks all covered in mud, she ate the grass growing there. Faced with this strange sight, the people exclaimed,

"Look what she's doing. She's mad!"

Bernadette was lifted up and smacked. She was taken to the judge who threatened to put her in prison if she continued with her nonsense. Bernadette replied in defence,

"I didn't do anything wrong... I promised to go there for fifteen days."

A small spring started to flow from the hole dug by Bernadette. People prayed with fervour at the grotto. Some people, imitating Bernadette, drank the water. A lady soaked her paralysed hand in it and then took it out of the water, completely healed. It was said to be a miracle.

After the thirteenth Apparition, Bernadette went to see Father Peyramale, the parish priest of Lourdes.

"The young lady asks that people come here in procession..."

The priest, cutting her short, raised his voice,

"Liar! It is his Lordship the Bishop who decides about processions."

And he showed her the door without listening to her anymore.

Vexed that she had not had time to say everything that the young lady had
asked for, the same evening, she returned to the priest,
"She also told me to go and tell the priests to build a chapel here... even a
very small one..."
Satisfied, she returned to the cachot, singing,
"I've done my errand... I've done my errand."

Bernadette returned several times to ask Father Peyramale to build a chapel but every time he replied,

"If she wants the chapel, tell her to say her name and make the rose bush, which grows at the entrance of the grotto, flower!"

For three weeks Bernadette no longer went to the grotto.

On Thursday 25th March, it was still dark when Bernadette woke up. A great sense of joy filled her heart.

She ran to the grotto. This was the sixteenth Apparition.

"Mademoiselle, would you be so kind as to tell me who you are, please?"

But all she had for a reply was a smile. Bernadette insisted. As the young lady laughed, Bernadette begged her,

"The priest would like to know your name..."

On the fourth request, the young lady put her hands together and raising her eyes towards heaven replied,

"I am the Immaculate Conception."

Bernadette ran as fast as she could to Father Peyramale,
"The young lady said: 'I am the Immaculate Conception!'"
The priest was astonished.
"A lady cannot have such a name, do you know what it means?"
"No!" said Bernadette.
"But that is what she said, I kept repeating it all the way here and she still wants the chapel."
Too overcome to explain to Bernadette what was meant by the Immaculate Conception, the priest sent Bernadette home. It was only that evening that she was at last told the truth. It really was the Blessed Virgin.

Several days later was the seventeenth Apparition. A disbelieving doctor was watching Bernadette as she prayed. The large candle which she was holding slipped and suddenly the flame touched her fingers but without hurting her. The doctor examined her hands. There was not a single burn! Astounded, he cried out for everyone to hear:

"Now I believe in it!"

Curiosity seekers, pilgrims and journalists arrived in crowds at Lourdes. Fearing disorder the police had a barricade put up, preventing entry to the Grotto.

On July16th, Bernadette once again felt the sensation of great joy in her heart which she knew so well. She went to the Grotto, her face hidden under a hood so as not be be recognised. Above the barriers, the young lady smiled at her. It was the eighteenth and last time that she saw the Blessed Virgin in this world. Amazed, she was to say,

"I have never seen her looking so beautiful... she has blue eyes."

People came from all around to see Bernadette. She was offered money to tell her story... but she would never accept it. She wanted to remain poor. In order to protect her from all these curiosity seekers, the parish priest allowed her to stay with the nuns at the hospital in Lourdes. There Bernadette learnt to take care of the poor and nurse the sick.

A statue of Our Lady of Lourdes was erected in the Grotto and the building of the chapel, which had been asked for by the Blessed Virgin, began.

Eight years later Bernadette was twenty two years old. She had decided to become a nun. Bernadette left her beloved parents and entered the convent of the sisters of Nevers. She was given the name of Sister Marie-Bernard. She became a nurse. She was to devote her life to nursing the sick and praying for sinners...

Her health was fragile however, and she became very ill. Three times she almost died. In spite of her sufferings she courageously continued her work for thirteen years. But the illness was stronger than her. Three days after Easter, suffering from terrible pains, Bernadette prayed,

"Holy Mary, mother of God, pray for me, poor sinner."

Then she asked for something to drink, like Jesus on the cross...

Having drunk, she inclined her head and very peacefully died.

Bernadette died at the age of thirty five on April 16th 1879.
Her marvellously preserved body was placed in a glass coffin. She can be seen in the chapel of the convent of Nevers.
She was proclaimed a Saint by Pope Pius XI.
Her feast day is celebrated every year on February 18th.
Since the Apparitions, Lourdes has attracted men and women from all over the world. Several basilicas and churches have been built to receive all the pilgrims: the Basilica of the Immaculate Conception, the Rosary Basilica, the underground Basilica of Saint Pius X and Saint Bernadette's Church...

Every year more than five million pilgrims come to pray to Our Lady of Lourdes in the Grotto of Massabielle. Many sick people have been cured: sixty-eight cures have been recognised as miracles.

Ⓞne day, you also will be happy to come to Lourdes, to pray in front of the
Grotto where Bernadette saw the Blessed Virgin, eighteen times.